THE GERMAN FALLSCHIRMJÄGER
IN WORLD WAR II

THE GERMAN FALLSCHIRMJÄGER IN WORLD WAR II

by Hauptmann Piehl
with a Foreword by
General der Flieger Kurt Student

Translated from the German by David Johnston

Schiffer Military History
Atglen, PA

Translated from the German by David Johnston.
This book was originally published under the title, *Ganze Männer* in 1943.

Copyright © 1997 by Schiffer Publishing Ltd. and William P. Moran.
Library of Congress Catalog Number: 96-70649.

Printed in the United States of America.
ISBN: 0-7643-0230-2

We are interested in hearing from authors with book ideas on related topics.

Published by Schiffer Publishing Ltd.
77 Lower Valley Road
Atglen, PA 19310
Phone: (610) 593-1777
FAX: (610) 593-2002
Please write for a free catalog.
This book may be purchased from the publisher.
Please include $2.95 postage.
Try your bookstore first.

The *Reichsmarschall* says:

"What you (the parachute troops) accomplished in the days before linking up with the advancing army is truly a heroic saga." (From a speech to the German press after the operation in Holland.)

"Our victory banners wave over Crete. You, my paratroopers and airborne troops....have....all ranks, under your proven leaders achieved unprecedented feats."

"Paratroopers: filled with an unstoppable offensive spirit, you, entirely on your own, defeated the numerically superior enemy in an heroic, bitter struggle. Wherever you landed you both stormed heroically and held stubbornly." (From an order of the day issued on 2 June 1941.)

General der Flieger Student

the Commanding General of the parachute and airborne troops on the morning of 10/5/1940 in his first command post during operations in Holland

"In the present struggle for the future of our people, the German parachute troops have on every front exhibited the best soldierly virtues, great offensive spirit, and most of all an unsurpassed willingness to sacrifice. Wherever they fought they were the terror of the enemy. England sees them as its mortal enemy!

May this description of the life of the individual paratrooper and of the training and victories of the German parachute corps reach the most isolated corners of Greater Germany and encourage our enthusiastic youth to join us."

The parachutist's badge.

The Song of the Paratroopers

1.
Red shines the sun, get ready, who knows
whether it will still smile for us tomorrow?
The engines start, full throttle,
takeoff, on our way, today we meet the enemy.
Into the aircraft, into the aircraft!
Comrade, there is no going back.
In the distant west there are dark clouds,
come along, and don't lose heart, come along!

2.
Thundering engines, alone with one's thoughts,
each one gives a quick thought to his loved ones at home,
then, comrades, comes the signal to jump,
and we drift towards the enemy, light the beacon fire there.
Quickly we land, quickly we land.
Comrade, there is no going back.
In the distant west there are dark clouds,
come along, don't lose heart, come along!

3.
Our numbers are small, our blood is wild,
we fear neither the enemy nor death,
we know just one thing: with Germany in distress,
to fight, to win, to die the death.
To your rifles, to your rifles!
Comrade, there is no going back.
In the distant west there are dark clouds,
come along, don't lose heart, come along!

Propaganda Service drawing: Baitz.

THE SOLDIERS OF
THE PARACHUTE CORPS

Periodically notices appear in the German daily newspapers whose contents are similar to the following:

"The Reich Minister of Aviation and the Commander-in-Chief of the Luftwaffe states that volunteers for the parachute corps are being accepted on a regular basis. They are to be directed to the responsible recruiting district headquarters."

The information that accompanies this notice states that recruits between the ages of 17 and 31 are preferred. Otherwise conditions for acceptance are the same as the other branches of the armed forces. Applicants who are already flight personnel will not be considered. Applicants can also apply for the non-commissioned officer plan with a twelve-year period of service.

The parachute corps, which demands the utmost of all its members, consists exclusively of volunteers. Everyone who decides to join this elite corps must be aware that physical, spiritual and moral demands will be made of him which are greater than those made of almost every other branch of the armed forces. Those who come to the parachute corps must thus be complete men. After a long and demanding period of training – only those in top physical and mental condition should apply – there beckons action, which demands of everyone the utmost courage and willingness to

sacrifice, but which is also rewarded with recognition of the highest degree. Men lacking a solid character, perhaps driven only by the lust for adventure, have no place in the parachute corps.

To describe the life and experiences of the young men in our parachute schools we now turn to two war correspondents, who, as members of the parachute corps themselves, of course received the same training as their comrades.

One war correspondent described in detail the training syllabus:

"If someone had told us during our high school days of a school whose curriculum required neither classes nor homework, but instead promised sport, sport and more sport, as well as flying and jumping – we would have considered such a school a pipe dream. And yet we found it – a school in which it is the upright fellow who gets through instead of the teacher's pet or the stay-at-home, the one always ready to try something new, with both feet on the ground even as a boy, who puts aside his books whenever the sun beckons him to the sports field, the swimming pool or a hike, and who nevertheless does his duty. You will meet them all today in our parachute schools – worker, student, artisan or farmer.

Instruction does not take place in a classroom. Big hangars and a landing field are its training grounds. The drone of aircraft engines and the bustle of an air base make the daily life of a budding paratrooper a young man's paradise.

13

Let us enter the first hangar. Its floor is almost covered with thick mats on which the recruits 'play around' (or so it seems to the layman). And yet all there is a serious purpose behind all this. Over there one group is engaged in 'rolling.' They are learning to end every fall in a roll. What is a roll? It is a new type of somersault, over the left or right shoulder, forwards or backwards.

The next group is engaged in an exercise in which they 'dive' over six men and then after flying over six backs turn their 'landing' into a roll. On the next mat is a tower with a ladder. Here the paratrooper trainees jump from a height of two meters and turn their landing into – a roll. They also practice jumping into a net to simulate leaving an aircraft. The jumpers climb ever higher in order to prolong as long as possible the feeling of soaring through the air. In the neighboring group the more advanced trainees hang from a suspension system that uses the same harness which will later hold them in their parachutes. They are raised up in this device and swung back and forth as on a swing. It is necessary to maintain the correct posture for a landing, for without warning the group instructor will release the suspended student. Now he must make the best possible landing. Sports equipment of every kind is available, for every student who passes through the stages of training in this hangar should come out of the preparatory sports school as hard as steel and flexible. These exercises turn even the 'most delicate little boy' into a sinewy jumper.

Not far from this hangar one might think he had been transported to an aircraft graveyard. On closer examination, however, one finds that the same section of the Ju 52, the aircraft used to transport the paratroopers, has been cut out – namely the 'belly', the part of the fuselage with the jump door. Here they practice jumping from the aircraft, with sawdust or peat moss taking the place of the air. Inside the mock-up, however, the trainees learn what they must do when the command 'get ready' is given, how they must attach their snap hooks to the static line and hold fast to the handles of the jump door before they dare stick their noses into the storm wing produced by the propellers. All this is practiced with the same meticulous caution that soldiers exercise in handling their weapons.

Having seen 'Ju's' without engines, wings and undercarriages, in the next hangar we find two more complete 'aircraft remains,' which, though no longer air worthy, still have their engines and undercarriage. Of course there are also special machines called 'wind donkeys'. Outside on the landing field one is now in use; as one can see there, the metal donkey's sole purpose is to create wind. The wind fills parachutes and its force blows them along the ground. This exercise is great fun for the trainees. While being dragged over the field by the parachute, they try to get to their feet, in order to run around the silk as quickly as possible so that it collapses and can no longer be caught by the wind.

Practicing the roll on the mat.

The jump and roll over ten men.

Taking the obstacle course with weapons and equipment.

Reinforced jump boots...

...knee protectors and wrappings...

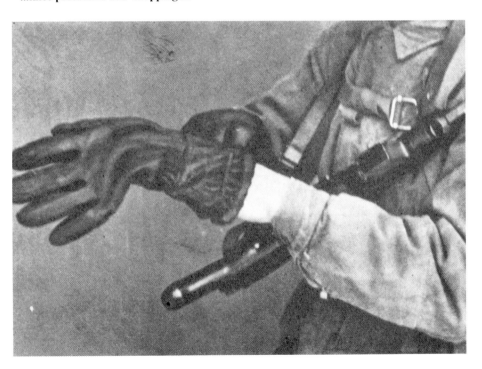

...and gloves protect the parachutist during the landing.

The packing hangar and parachute stores form a complex all their own. Hundreds of special long tables are required, for each paratrooper must learn to pack his own chute; servicing, drying and caring for the parachutes takes a great deal of space. To the beginner packing at first seems an arcane skill – the process of turning the maze of silk and lines into the small package of a ready to use parachute is a complicated one. However, after a few days, using the Wehrmacht's tested teaching method, a trainee who at first required perhaps half a day to pack a parachute can now accomplish the task in less than an hour. Constant observation by the responsible superior as well as precisely specified interim checks at the end of each step of the packing process ensure that each parachute is packed according to regulations.

In front of the hangar is the place where the rules of an equally comprehensive and meticulous training process prove themselves – the jump field. There the trainees who have completed their basic training wait feverishly for their first jump. Before they are allowed to take off, however, their instructors, the group training officer and the assistant group training officer, led by the company commander, climb into the aircraft to demonstrate how it is done – as on every course – to their students. The aircraft take off and after reaching a certain height the paratroopers suddenly leap from the doors of the transport

The "wind donkey" at work.

machine. The trainees see the spectacle of parachute after parachute opening, bearing the jumpers slowly and safely to earth. Soon afterward, when the young paratroopers make their first jump, they experience for themselves the most gripping experience the German Air Force can give its soldiers: jumping from the sky.

Those who have experienced it are – like all paratroopers – sworn to this corps with all the enthusiasm of a young man who saw a danger facing him, approached it courageously, and realized that for the brave it was in fact no danger."

Another war correspondent gave a graphic account of his first parachute jump:

"Probably never before has the start of a takeoff seemed so slow and methodical. Nor has it ever been so windy. But that is good, for the cool draft has something wonderfully stimulating about it. How long have we been airborne? It has only been minutes and yet it seems to me much, much longer until the oft-practiced and familiar commands for the jump ring out. Thus, too, is the final uncertainty overcome. Now one must pay close attention, most of all to jump properly and safely in one's own interest! But there is also the threat of criticism by the instructors, whose sharp eyes carefully follow every move-

"To the aircraft."

Static lines between their teeth, the men climb into their Ju.

ment by their students from above in the aircraft and from below at the landing site. Not just for self-satisfaction does each man try to jump correctly, but also to land without being hurt. Every mistake during the jump and the landing means more sweat for the trainee parachutist, embodied in the term 'ground exercises.' Therefore there is little time for final fearful emotions before the jump.

Tense anticipation before the first jump.

The command 'get ready' is given, the snap hooks locked in place. The great moment has come and it seizes me. All thoughts now are concentrated on the jump. 'Ready to jump' and step into the door. I look straight ahead at the left wing. I must not miss the signal to jump, so as not to give the impression of hesitating. The full force of the wind strikes my cheeks. Every nerve is on edge. They must have been able to see my face, for afterward my comrades told me that it had a totally different, new expression. The signal to jump is given – push down hard with both legs, arms thrust into the air and – out. Away from the aircraft. Earlier we had bet that each man would yell 'let's go!', with the slipstream from the aircraft a doubtful undertaking. Everyone, including me, claimed to have shouted, but nothing could be heard.

The parachute opens in seconds, so quickly that one doesn't know what is happening on the first jump. Later it is different, for experience makes a big difference and ultimately one waits from minute to minute for the shock of deployment, which is larger or smaller depending on the skill of the jumper.

The slipstream disfigures the jumper's face.

Then the jump...

But back to the first jump, the first experience of swaying safely in the air, the beautiful feeling of rebirth experienced by a man with all senses alive. Beneath us the earth. Comrades float beside me. One would like to shout out loud for joy, to express the tremendous feeling of happiness which the most flowery superlatives cannot describe. Words are not enough, one has to read the faces of the men to fully grasp the experience of the first and most beautiful jump. If parachute jumping were a sport and not one of the proudest accomplishments by a German soldier, no other sport in the world could compare with it. What do all other experiences, accomplishments or joys have to offer the parachutist to equal this unique experience of mastery of the air? Only one wish remains: let this floating last a long time.

But the earth approaches in giant steps and with it the landing, which is also watched and criticized, for the safe arrival of a soldier ready to fight depends on it. Once again astonishment at the adaptability of the well-trained body to meet the demands of landing on the ground. There is nothing that cannot be drilled into a soldier by practice and more practice so that every nerve and limb reacts automatically.

...and the parachute bears the jumper to the earth.

A textbook landing.

This parachutist found the time to photograph himself.

Feet together. A short bounce, my body contracts to roll forwards (or backwards) and soon I am standing again on what is now once more firm and safe mother earth. Just like on the practice field I run after my chute, release the harness and with the help of my nearest comrade recover my parachute. Then it is away quickly to clear the area, hand over my parachute and report to the company commander and chief instructor. Gratitude for his training can be seen in the eyes of all the men, and his success and that of his instructors is shown in the sound limbs of all his students. For us this day is one to celebrate. He has given us an experience that comes only once and we all can only wish that many German men might be granted the same experience."

After training at the parachute school the new paratrooper arrives at his replacement-training or operational unit, where he is given the final polish before going into action and receives the beautiful emblem with the diving eagle. Parachute jumping is after all just a means to an end, to a certain degree no more than a means of transporting a soldier close to his actual end, the battle. The paratrooper receives the best possible training.

The instructor uses a megaphone to shout corrections.

The paratrooper becomes familiar with and learns to use a wide range of weapons and equipment, which enable him not just to take an enemy position, but also to hold stubbornly until relieved by ground troops.

The armament and equipment used by the paratrooper are designed for this role and they have been thoroughly tested and evaluated.

Over the usual Luftwaffe uniform the soldier wears the familiar outfit consisting of shirt and pants. His hands and knees are protected by jumper's gloves and knee guards; foot wrappings and special boots are intended to prevent injuries while jumping. The paratrooper helmet has a thick foam-rubber lining; the shape of the steel helmet, which

Mass drop involving a large number of transports.

differs from the standard armed forces model, immediately identifies the soldier as a paratrooper. The belt, the gas mask, the cartridge pouches, two rations bags and two canteens complete the equipment carried on the body.

Packed in their own containers, the weapons accompany the men to the scene of the action and are dropped with them.

Having so far spoken only of the trainee soldiers, here a word of thanks to the paratrooper instructors.

Paratroopers also learn to
use the range-finder.

Paratrooper-engineers during a river crossing.

With a heavy cable drum on his back, the signals soldier lays down necessary lines of communication.

Smoking out a bunker.

Officers and non-commissioned officers who instruct one course after another are performing a highly responsible service, one which involves personal sacrifice, especially in time of war. Although the instructors have to be among the most capable of the paratroopers, never or rarely are they permitted to see combat. The men who are trained to be paratroopers by the instructors experience combat in the field, something the former know only in theory. True the instructors know that their work contributes to the winning of battles, but this knowledge is not enough to completely satisfy them. But it is said that no paratrooper ever forgets his instructor. In the toughest actions the example of the instructor appears before a fighting man and remembering him often helps master even the most difficult situations.

Practicing with the heavy machine-gun.

Propaganda Service drawing: Baitz.

The Paratrooper's Faithful "Comrades"

In addition to the weapons which the paratrooper needs to fight, which have already been mentioned, his most important helper is the parachute, which bears him to the earth after he has jumped from the transport aircraft.

The idea of the parachute is very old. The famous artist Leonardo da Vinci was probably the first to concern himself with designing a parachute, in the 15th Century. Whether or not he tested it in practice is unknown. After experiments by other inventors, which failed to yield satisfactory results, in 1777 Joseph Montgolfier, the inventor of the hot air balloon, made a parachute jump from the roof of his house. In the following period he repeated the experiment. Jumps from greater heights were only possible after the invention of the balloon. The Frenchman Blanchard became the first man to use a parachute in an emergency situation in the air in 1785. Several years later the parachute, which until then was extremely primitive by modern standards, was improved by adding an air outlet at the apex of the parachute, thereby solving the problem of serious oscillations during descent. A whole series of inventors experimented with parachutes during the course of the

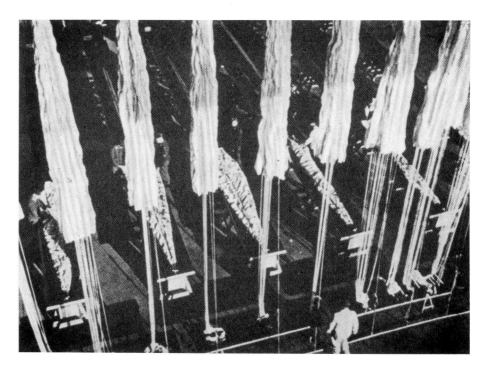

Parachutes in the drying and packing hangar.

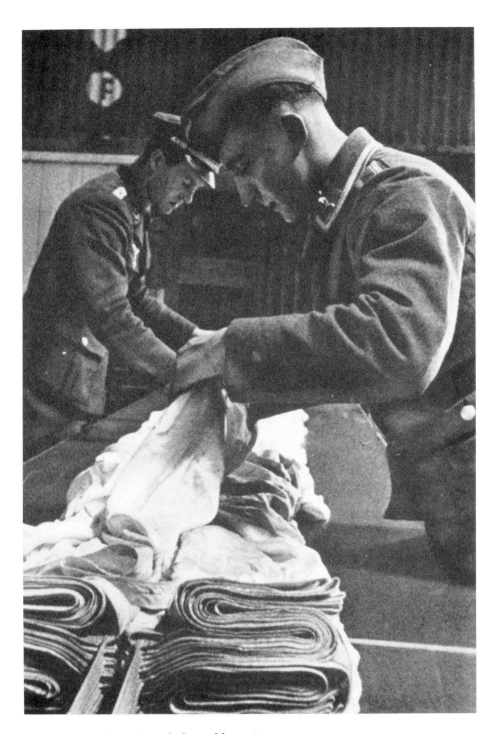

The packing of parachutes is done with great care.

decade; beginning in 1890 Germans Käthe Paulus and Paul Lattemann introduced fundamental improvements. All these parachutes could be used for jumping from balloons but not from aircraft moving at high speeds. A design that could was produced in 1917 by the German Heinecke, who was involved with airships. He connected the parachute to the aircraft by means of a static line, which opened the parachute after the jumper was a sufficient distance away from the aircraft. The first "manual" parachute was developed in 1919; this parachute could be opened by the jumper when he chose to by pulling a release handle.

The designers of the German service parachute, which is used by the entire parachute corps, did everything humanly possible to ensure the safety of the jumper. Only the very best materials are used in the factories; it must undergo numerous checks before it reaches the machines where it receives its final form. Frequent strength tests ensure that the parachute can bear several times the weight of a grown man.

• • •

The paratroopers' transport aircraft, the Junkers Ju 52, is so well known, not just in Germany but throughout the entire world, that any words would be superfluous. The German command realized in time what great value this aircraft would have in wartime as a transporter of troops and material and saw to it that it was placed into quantity production. In this way it was possible to launch and successfully execute large-scale parachute operations. Obviously this machine is used for more than just carrying parachute troops into combat. It has also performed invaluable services in delivering all manner of supplies, whether food, munitions, weapons or fuel, and continues to do so. Countless wounded sing its praises; many of our paratroopers, too, owe their lives and health to the Ju 52 air ambulance.

• • •

And now a word about the medical services of the parachute corps. The creators of the corps realized that its special character and purpose would also require specialized medical personnel. In each parachute operation, therefore, sufficiently large medical units were dropped, and these cared for the sick and wounded during the heaviest fighting. Their courageous efforts were acknowledged by the awarding of two Knight's Crosses (*Oberfeldarzt* Dr. Neumann and *Oberstabsarzt* Dr. Jäger) and numerous other high decorations.

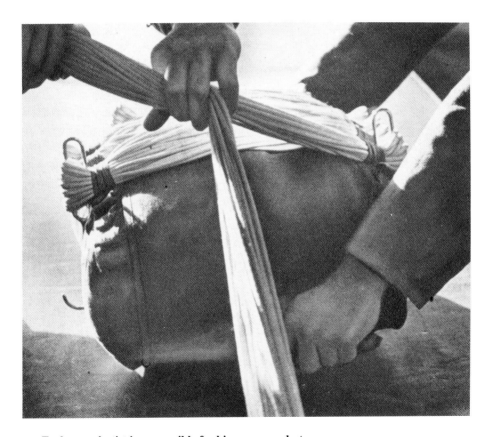

Each parachutist is responsible for his own parachute.

Propaganda Service drawing: Baitz.

The Ju also carries heavy loads.

The History of the Parachute Corps
Abroad and in Germany

America

America has been the scene of important work in the field of parachute development since the 1880's. Parachute jumping was taken up there, though more for reasons of sensation seeking, and was presented as entertainment.

In April 1928 a sergeant and ten men of the Army's air weapons school carried out the "first mass jump in history." It is no wonder, therefore, that the Russians sought to follow this American example.

Even though the Americans were on the right track from the very beginning, and even though some military leaders recognized the importance of parachute troops, supporters of a parachute corps were unable to push through their plans. Leadership in this field thus passed to Russia, and it was not until after the success of the German parachute forces in Belgium and Holland in 1940 that a true parachute corps was formed in the USA.

Soviet Russia

The Soviet Armed Forces were the first to recognize the military value of parachute troops. Already in 1929 the military pilot Minov was sent to America to study the science of the parachute. The next year in Russia, in 1930, a group trained by him made the first mass jump. Soviet Russia conducted an experimental program with jumps under the widest range of conditions, such as from the maximum and minimum possible heights. Parachute jumping became a national sport and jump towers were set up in even the smallest towns. From the very beginning all experiments and tests have been aimed at military applications. By 1931 there were already several battalions of paratroopers. In September 1935 1,200 paratroopers were used in maneuvers near Kiev, 2,200 near Moscow. In terms of numbers and experience the Soviets thus had a huge lead over the rest of the world in the field of parachute jumping. Russian parachutists held numerous records, and its specialists built on a broad mass of parachutists.

Nevertheless Soviet Russia was incapable of exploiting this lead, probably because of the wave of purges in the army which caused the most capable heads to roll, including Marshall Tukhachevsky. The first use of parachute troops in earnest – during the Finnish campaign – was weak and ineffective.

France

Obviously impressed by the success of Soviet parachute troops during maneuvers, in 1935 the French founded a parachute school at Pujaut-Avignon and began building a French parachute corps. Two paratrooper companies were formed in 1936; on 21 August 1937 French paratroopers were used as a demolition squad in maneuvers. Subsequently, however, little was done with the French parachute troops. According to the former French minister of aviation P. Cot, they were rejected by the general staff as a "circus act" and disbanded.

Italy

The Italian parachute corps was formed even later than the French corps in summer 1936 following the experience of the Abyssinian campaign. Italian parachute troops were used with success in 1941 during the Greek campaign, occupying the Ionian islands.

Great Britain

In England a parachute corps was apparently first established on a broad basis in 1940 following the success of German parachute troops in Holland. This process took place in the British Isles and in the Empire, in Canada and India, for example. Parachute formations were also formed from emigrant personnel – Czechs, Poles, French, Dutch, etc. The English stressed the value of parachutists as saboteurs and no serious parachute operations were undertaken in the first three years of the war.

Summing up, therefore, it can be said that America led the way in the field of parachuting until about 1930, but then for the next 6 to 8 years leadership passed to the Soviet Union. From about 1935 the success enjoyed in maneuvers by the Soviet parachute troops attracted the attention of almost all the major states, however most progressed no farther in their development than experimental units.

Germany

From the very beginning Germany made significant contributions to the development of the parachute and experiments in parachute jumping. During the First World War some brave men successfully used parachutes to land behind the enemy lines. Restricted after the war, the German Armed Forces were of course in no position to compete with the experimental programs being pursued by America and Soviet Russia.

The revitalized new Germany not only recognized the importance of this new weapon but also possessed the strength to make it its own. Orders were issued for the formation of a German parachute corps. The first parachute jumps by the Luftwaffe to be held in public took place in autumn 1936 during the harvest festival on the Bückeberg. One year later parachute troops took part in the armed forces maneuvers. By another year later, in autumn 1938, the German parachute corps was already strong enough to make a significant and successful contribution to the occupation of the Sudetenland and then in March 1939 to the occupation of Prague.

Soon afterwards, on 20 April 1939, units of the young, proud parachute corps for the first time participated in the parade to mark the Führer's birthday, to the applause of the crowds.

In 1936 the Luftwaffe publicly demonstrated parachute jumping on the occasion of the harvest festival on the Bückeberg.

The young parachute corps in the Sudetenland.

Paratroopers take part in the march into Prague.

Paratrooper units during the great parade to mark the Führer's birthday in 1939. Today the flag bearer wears the Knight's Cross.

THE YOUNG CORPS PROVES
ITSELF IN ACTION

Poland, Denmark, Norway

When several months later in 1939 war came, the German parachute troops were of course involved from the beginning. Fighting in the role of infantry, they played a successful role in several battles in Poland.

They took part in the occupation of Denmark.

In Norway they fought heroically at Oslo, Stavanger, Dombas and Narvik. It was in Norway that the parachute troops won their first Knight's Crosses.

Belgium and Holland

However, the parachute corps' first large-scale and most decisive operation was to come during the offensive in the west. On 10 May 1940 German paratroops landed in Belgium and took the bridges over the Albert Canal and the fortress of Eben Emael, part of the fortifications of Liége. In command of the paratroopers was the then *Hauptmann* Koch; a specially trained assault group was led by the then *Oberleutnant* Witzig. Both officers received the Knight's Cross.

A tiny force overran, defeated or captured a vastly superior number of defenders or at least held them in check until units of the German Army arrived and relieved the paratroopers.

Propaganda Service drawing: Baitz.

Propaganda Service drawing: Baitz.

One of the enemy's most dangerous fortifications had been put out of action. The bridges, destruction of which would have seriously held up the German advance, fell into our hands intact. Belgium's defeat came so quickly that the English and French had no time to come to her aid as they had planned.

In Holland, too, the use of paratroops and air-landed forces, which were under the personal command of *Generalleutnant* Student, upset the enemy's plans from the outset. The huge air transport operation was carried out under the command of *Oberst* Conrad and *Oberstleutnant* Wilke. On 10 May 1940 paratroops descended on the Waalhaven airfield, captured it and made it possible for the troop transports to land.

Other elements took the Nieuwe-Maas bridges in Rotterdam, the Oude-Maas bridge near Dordrecht and the major bridges near Moerdijk. These forces were commanded by *Oberst* Bräuer. All the captured positions held out for days against heavy attacks. The paratroopers paralyzed enemy movements, tied down very strong forces and prevented the bridges from being blown.

Polish prisoners of war taken by German paratroopers.

As they had done in Belgium, in Holland too their efforts enabled the German Army to advance through that country unhindered. The use of German parachute troops thus played a significant role in the surrender of Belgium and Holland and ultimately also created the necessary conditions for the rapid defeat of France.

After the victories in the east and north, in the west parachute forces made a decisive contribution to a campaign for the first time in history. From a weapon whose practicality was still in dispute in the rest of the world, German research, energy and organization had created a corps which had now demonstrated that it led the world in its field.

Paratroopers come to the aid of their hard-pressed comrades.

Landing in the snow and ice in Norway.

Head-first leap toward the landing cross.

At a Norwegian railroad station.

The Albert Canal also formed a part of the Belgian system of fortifications.

Men such as these forced it as well as...

...the "strongest fort in the world" Eben Emael.

The Führer too is grateful.

At the gates of Fortress Holland paratroopers took...

...the Moerdijk bridges and...

...secured them for our advancing panzer units.

56

Greece (Corinth and Crete)

Now, with the English driven from the mainland, and with German men standing guard from the North Cape to the Bay of Biscay, the British tried to reenter Europe through the back door. They landed in Greece and in Yugoslavia they succeeded in upsetting the good relations that Germany had cultivated there and turned certain circles against Germany.

So Germany was forced into the Balkans campaign, which began on 6 April 1941 and led to the surrender of the Serbian Army on 17th April.

In Greece, after the capture of Saloniki and Larissa one of the most important strategic points was Corinth. The small bridges over the canal there constituted the sole line of communication, including road, rail and telephone, between the Peloponnese and the mainland.

Corinth Canal, which was taken by our parachute troops.

This point had to be of great importance to the British retreat. Therefore, on 26 April 1941, paratroopers under the command of Oberst Sturm jumped far in advance of the army and took the canal and the city of Corinth, captured a large haul of booty, and in British prisoners alone took a number which far exceeded their own. The next day they took Argos and Nauplia.

The British had thus been driven from the mainland.

The sole part of Greece still in British hands was Crete. They knew that, in German hands, it would be very dangerous for their position in Africa and in the Mediterranean. On the other hand, in the hands of the English this bulwark in the Mediterranean posed a

Generaloberst Löhr during a conversation with Oberst Sturm.

Weapons captured in and near Corinth...

...Greek prisoners of war...

...and British.

Parade in Athens.

severe threat to the Greek mainland and German-Italian shipping routes across the Mediterranean. The island therefore had to be taken, even though a strong defense by the English had to be expected.

Without the parachute troops the mission could not be carried out. They were therefore assembled in Greece and went into action from there on the morning of 20 May 1941.

For the assault *General* Student formed groups which jumped and fought under *Generalmajor* Meindl near the Malemes airfield in the west of the island, under *Generalleutnant* Süßmann and after his death in a crash under *Oberst* Heidrich near Khania, under *Oberst* Sturm near Rethimnon, and finally under *Oberst* Bräuer near Iraklion.

By jumping at different places into the midst of a superior enemy, the latter's movements were immediately severed at the main points and paralysed.

General der Flieger Student and General Ringel discuss the Crete operation.

The paratroopers get ready for takeoff.

Furthermore the Malemes airfield was taken in heavy fighting; beginning on 21st May alpine troops were landed there and together with them the island was rolled up from the west. On 27th May Khania, the capital of Crete, was taken, Rethimnon on 29th May and Iraklion on 30th may. By 2 June 1941 the conquest of Crete was largely concluded. For the first time in history an island, and moreover a strongly fortified and stoutly defended one, had fallen to an attack from the sky. Not only had the parachute troops held their own against a vastly superior force, but in the end they defeated it. Apart from his heavy losses in dead and wounded, the enemy also lost 12,000 men captured; as well the German forces released 14,000 Italian prisoners of war.

A large number of transports carry them to the rocky island in the Mediterranean.

Landing and...

...combat on Crete.

Many German aircraft on the fiercely-contested Malemes airfield.

A captured British tent camp near Khania.

Paratroopers amid the thousands of prisoners taken by them.

Soldiers of the parachute corps describe their battle for the benefit of the commanding general...

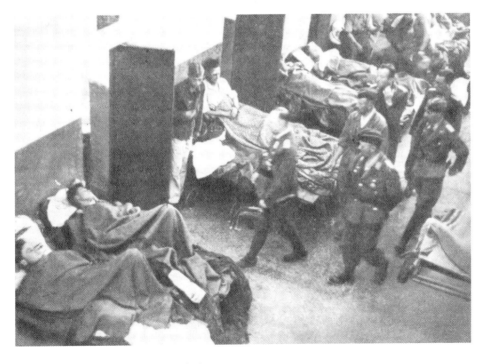

...who visits the wounded in hospital.

Mass jump.

Cretan donkeys carried the paratroopers' weapons and equipment.

On foot...

...and in captured vehicles, the advance went on until...

...the surrender of individual cities and the capture of the entire island.

Watch on the Mediterranean.

In the East 1941-1943

In jumping into areas held by the enemy the parachute corps had proved that it totally deserved the trust placed in it and that it was the decisive instrument of the German command that the latter thought it was.

In Germany the units were brought up to strength and soon they were ready for action again.

On the eastern front, when bolshevism thought it could defeat the German Army with the help of "General Winter", the parachute troops were committed to fight off the mass assaults by the Asiatics together with their comrades of the army. At the hot spots of these tremendous winter battles the men of the parachute, this time as ground troops, renewed the fame they had earned on the various fronts. Wherever they were the Soviets received a bloody nose; they launched powerful counterattacks which retook important strongpoints and the Russian winter was no more able to diminish their thirst for action than had the tropical heat on Crete. Everywhere they performed truly heroic deeds. They stood shoulder to shoulder with the troops of the various We*hrmacht* elements and their selfless actions saw to it that the Soviets did not achieve their goal, the overrunning of the German front. The Commander-in-Chief of one army in whose formations parachute troops fought said of them: "Superior in their discipline, toughness and training, with an exemplary spirit of cooperation they fought, bled and triumphed at the side of the army."

Alarm on the Neva Front near Leningrad.

Paratroopers on skis in the vastness of Russia.

The brief summer months were used to retrain the units and bring them up to strength. For most of the corps this took place in northern France. The paratroopers were very sorry that they were unable to see action at Dieppe, where a landing attempt by the English went totally awry. Although they were nearby they did not see action – so quickly was this adventure by Mr. Churchill ended. But it was not just in the east that the parachute troops proved themselves during this "jumpless" period.

Parachutist troubleshooter at his difficult work.

Waiting for the Soviets to attack, in an ice bunker...

...or in a foxhole.

Mortar fire on the Soviet positions.

Generalfeldmarschall Rommel and General Ramcke at the command post in North Africa.

North Africa, Tunis

Under the command of *Generalmajor* Ramcke, a parachute brigade was formed that was sent to North Africa. It was assigned a sector on the southern wing of the El Alamein position which bordered the Qattara Depression. In attack and defense, under the hardest living conditions in the African desert sun, here too German parachute troops lived up to the expectations placed in them. And when it became necessary for the German-Italian panzer army to withdraw to the west before the numerically superior enemy, the Ramcke Brigade held its positions to the very end. Encircled by powerful enemy forces, it succeeded in making a much talked about breakout to reach Rommel's army.

In true paratrooper style, in the course of the breakout the unit captured enough enemy vehicles that the brigade, which was not a motorized unit, was able to drive straight across the desert in British trucks to reach the army. The *Führer* rewarded this daring act by awarding the unit's leader the Oak Leaves to go with the Knight's Cross he had won on Crete.

Americans and their allies may have been surprised when the first German troops they met in Tunisia were also paratroopers. There, and later in Sicily, they fought stubbornly for every foot of ground and inflicted heavy losses on the enemy.

So this rounds out the picture of the German parachute troops in the first years of the war. We have seen them on every front, on every front they have proved themselves. They have performed acts of courage that will figure prominently in the history of the war. The fame that this young corps has added to its banners is immortal. From all that has been said, it is obvious that they will continue to go wherever the *Führer*'s order calls them and will have an important say in the outcome of every battle.

In one paragraph of the *Duties of the German Soldier* it says:

"The soldier's honor lies in the unconditional commitment of his person for V*olk und Vaterland* to the sacrificing of his life."

Many of our paratroopers have paid the ultimate price demanded by this voluntary oath. Whether in the far north of Norway or in the eternal sands of the African deserts, whether death came in the struggle in the west, on Crete, or in the endless expanses of Russia, everywhere their hero's graves offer proof of their unconditional commitment of their person. But their sacrifice is neither useless nor forgotten. Each of them lives in the memory of their surviving comrades who still fight on. All of these dead are a reminder and an example for the entire parachute corps and shall be for all the young Germans who join its ranks.

On the march under the African sun.

A paratrooper's "bed" in the desert.

Paratroopers were the first German troops in Tunisia.

In good cover.

Arabs help the paratroops get their bearings in the approaches to Tunis.

French policeman in conversation with paratroopers.

A lonely tent in the Tunisian mountain land.

We had a good comrade.

Monument to the parachute troops on Crete.

Ready for the next mission.

The Reward for Courage in Action

...is shown in few words by a list of the decorations awarded so far.
Members of the parachute corps and its transport units have won:

The Knight's Cross of the Iron Cross with Oak Leaves 1
The Knight's Cross of the Iron Cross 61
The German Cross in Gold 56
The Iron Cross, First Class .... ca. 5,000
The Iron Cross, Second Class .... ca. 17,000
The War Merit Cross, First Class 42
The War Merit Cross, Second Class .... a. 3,100

As well a large number of goblets and salvers of honor have been awarded and other recognitions given.

Decorations for deserving soldiers of the parachute corps.

General der Flieger Student presents several of his Knight's Cross wearers to the Reichsmarschall.

As well as the Commanding General of the Parachute and Airborne Corps, General der Flieger Student, the following wear the Knight's Cross of the Iron Cross:

for action in

GenLt. Ramcke	Crete
	Oak Leaves North Africa
Major Altmann	Albert Canal
Lt. Arpke	Albert Canal (KIA)
Hptm. Barmetler	Crete
Hptm. Becker	Crete
Oblt. Graf Blücher	Holland (KIA)
GenLt. Bräuer	Holland
GenMaj. Conrad	Holland
Hptm. Delica	Eben Emael
Major Egger	Crete
Oblt. Fulda	Corinth-Crete
Hptm. Genz	Corinth-Crete
Major Gericke	Corinth-Crete
Feldw. Görtz	Holland
Oblt. Hagl	Crete
GenLt. Heidrich	Crete
Oberstlt. Heilmann	Crete
Major Herrmann	Crete

Major v.d. Heydte	Crete
Oblt. Höfeld	North Africa
Major Ingenhoven	Norway (KIA)
Oberstabsarzt Dr. Jäger	Albert Canal
Feldw. Kempke	Crete
Hptm. Kerfin	Holland (KIA)
Major Kieß	Albert Canal
Oberstlt. Koch	Eben Emael
Oberstlt. Kroh	Crete
GenMaj. Meindl	Crete
Hptm. Meißner	Albert Canal
Lt. Mischke	North Africa
Oberst Morzik	Eastern Front
Oberfeldarzt Dr. Neumann	Crete
Oberfeldw. Orth	Eastern Front (KIA)
Major Prager	Holland (KIA)
Oblt. Rapräger	North Africa
Hptm. Ringler	Holland
General Staff Major von Roon	Crete-Corinth
Lt. Sassen	Eastern Front

Hptm. Schacht	Albert Canal
Hptm. Schächter	Eben Emael
Major Schirmer	Corinth
Hptm. Schmidt	Dombas
Major Graf v.d. Schulenburg	Eastern Front
Oberstlt. Schulz	Holland
Lt. Schuster	Crete (KIA)
Hptm. Schwarzmann	Holland
Major Stentzler	Crete (KIA)
Hptm. Straehler-Pohl	North Africa
GenMaj. Sturm	Corinth-Crete
Oblt. Teusen	Corinth
Hptm. Tietjen	Holland
Hptm. Toschka	Crete
Oblt. Trebes	Crete
General Staff Oberst Trettner	Holland
Oblt. Wagner	Crete
Oberstlt. Walther	Holland
Oberfeldw. Welskop	Crete
Oberst Wilke	Holland
Major Witzig	Eben Emael
Major Zierach	Albert Canal